LIVE DIFFERENT MOMENTS

Elaine J. Clinger Sturtz

LIVE DIFFERENT MOMENTS

Elaine J. Clinger Sturtz

DECLARATION PRESS

Live Different Moments

Cover design by Steven Fisher, MFA.

Photography by Samantha Westling

ISBN 979-8-9891257-0-8

In Memory

In Memory of Annie, my companion and therapy dog.
Run free in Heaven, Annie Girl!

Dedication

Dedicated to all my counseling clients with whom I have walked the journey of life attempting to help them find hope and peace.
Dedicated to all widows and widowers who are trying to live in this different life they did not choose.
To the glory of God who is my strength, my redeemer, my companion in this different life.

Contents

Acknowledgements

Thank you to Mrs. Charlotte Leeth who was my editor and has also lived life to the fullest. Mrs. Leeth was my 9th Grade English teacher who encouraged me to write. I credit my writing career to her, but she just says, "It was in you. I just encouraged it to come out." Charlotte, at age ninety-five, lives life to the fullest and always lives in the moments in front of her. She is an inspiration!

Thank you to my cover designer, Steven Fisher, MFA. Steve was a youth in the first church I served as Associate Minister. He drew cartoons of me at Work Camp. Steve is an amazing artist. Website: FisherArtworks.com. Email: Fish@FisherArtworks.com.

Thank you to Samantha Westling and her gift of photography. Sam was in one of my youth groups, and I have watched her grow into an amazing young woman. God has blessed her with a wonderful talent. She has her own photography business – Humble + Kind Photography, LLC. Email: Samanatha@humbleandkind photography.com.

Introduction to Book

In my book, *Living In The Different,* I shared my grief journey and focused on the grief, the emotions, the changes, the memories, and the steps leading into the different life many of you now are experiencing. Grief mingles sorrow and joy, and memories and pain. Grief is filled with tears and loneliness, but it also includes hope and love. Love never ends and the love becomes integrated into your foundation of life. You stay in grief to process the past. Life is different and as you go through the grief process and begin to see a possibility of life again, you attempt to figure out who you are now after having experienced this deep loss. Life has changed.

The next chapter of life begins after the intensity of loss. You have recognized you are different and wonder how you will find this new life and truly live. Is it even possible to build a life again? Now that you are in this different life because of your loss, you begin to see a future that seems so difficult to step into and do more than just function and exist. "Now what do I do? Now who am I? Now how do I live in this different life?"

Each chapter and change makes life different. After my husband, Dave died, I had a faithful companion, my sweet beagle dog, Annie, to continue the journey. She became my constant companion. We helped each other in our grief and how to live in this different life. We had a special bond, and our hearts were connected on a deep level because of the loss. It was like we understood one another and served and sacrificed for each other. I learned more about the fullness of life and how to manage the different through my dog. I never did anything without her. Annie was always with me in every move and change.

Sometimes the responsibility of caring for her every need felt heavy, but I always loved her as my faithful companion. Now that I have had to release her to run in Heaven, I realize that I have learned how to live in the different with her. But how do I live differently without her? New chapter. New experience. New book.

Is it really possible to live differently in this world in your current life with all the changes? Could you? Do you want to? Life may be familiar and comfortable right now, but you feel empty, alone, overwhelmed with no meaning or purpose. You make it through each day, but you are just existing and surviving. That's great at first on the grief journey, but as life goes on, is it really enough?

As a Christian Counselor, I have listened to many people struggle with how to live life and find purpose and meaning because they have walls and roadblocks. Some of these roadblocks may include fear of failure, fear of the unknown, anxiety, doubt, focusing too far into the future, and the list is endless. They all desire to take steps, but it seems impossible. It seemed impossible to live life without my husband, Dave, but Annie was with me. She became my own therapy dog. Now it seems impossible to live this different life without my faithful companion.

Therefore, the creation of this book was to help me personally figure out how to live differently and to give you the opportunity to follow along with me on my journey. Annie is going to help us. Her life story is interwoven through each chapter and will help us to live differently, really!

Remember, different is not bad, it is just different. It is the completion of a relationship on earth. The love and influence continue and becomes part of the foundation of life. Because of all those who have influenced, guided, and been part of our lives, we are farther down the path of life. They are signposts to direct the journey. Annie will be our signpost to guide and direct you and me to live different and to actually live the fullness of life that Jesus calls us to live.

This is not just a new chapter in my life, it is a new book. Annie has helped me prepare for this new book of my life. She walked with me in the grief and was the familiar character that bridges the books. Annie did not allow anything or anyone to change the essence of who God created her to be. She adapted to situations and because of her own trauma and grief, became more compassionate and sensitive to the hurt and pain of others. Annie taught me not to change for others but be who God created me to be. Annie was part of the last book, and she has released me to enter this new and different life. This new book may have different characters – people I will draw closer to and different adventures.

I have a new freedom that comes from the loss. My priorities have changed because of the loss. My foundation is stronger because of all the love and influence from the completion of the past chapters of my life. I tried to fix and create a new life on my own believing I was strong enough to do it. I have found that I need Jesus to lead and guide me. I am focusing on glorifying God and living in His Presence each moment. My desire is to live in front of me whatever God has for me.

We cannot put who we were into this new book. Jesus spoke exactly to this when He said, *"And no one pours new wine into old wineskins. If he does, the wine will burst the skins, and both the wine and the wineskins will be ruined. No, he pours new wine into new wineskins." Mark 2:22 (NIV)* You cannot put your new life into the old way of life. You cannot live the same way you did before your loss. You are different. Your life is different. This is a new book. Change your focus. It is time to experience life differently. I am. Are you with me on this adventure?

Walk with me into this new book of life as God holds our hand! May you find the peace and contentment God has for you!

Introduction to Annie

I grew up on a farm with animals – cows, sheep, chickens, pigs, cats, and always a dog who lived outside in a doghouse. In my marriage, Specs came into my life. He was a tri-colored beagle who won my heart and lived in our home and sometime slept in our bed. For sixteen years, Specs was my faithful, patient, constant buddy. He was well-known in our neighborhood and among friends. Specs grew old and at sixteen years old crossed over the bridge into Heaven. I thought I would never love another dog like I loved Specs.

Several months later, my sister asked if I was interested in another dog. She sent me a picture of the cutest six-month-old beagle puppy. Who can resist the eyes of a beagle puppy? Her eyes even then seemed to look deep within my soul. Did I really want to have another dog and the responsibility of caring for a pet? Dave had retired and was eager to have a companion with him during the day while I worked. I knew as we drove to just look at the puppy, that she would be coming home with us. We adopted Annie on our

Anniversary and therefore named her "Annie" which was short for Anniversary.

Annie was born in a dog pound in Kenton, Ohio on June 24, 2012. Someone adopted her when she was old enough to be, but she was brought back to the pound a few weeks later. She was abandoned and not wanted. She was then rescued by a dog rescue group and named "Carmel apple." She lived in a barn with big dogs just outside my hometown. The lady who ran this rescue, Pat, felt sorry for her being the only small dog in a large dog rescue barn. Pat would often bring her into her house during the day to give her special attention. My sister saw Pat's post on Facebook that she was seeking someone to adopt this little beagle dog. I contacted Pat and set up a time to see this little beagle dog. We drove to my hometown knowing we would be bringing her home.

She was in the house when we arrived. When I sat down, Annie jumped into my lap and looked me in the eyes and licked my face. Annie chose me immediately. It was like she knew I was there to rescue her. We bonded. God knew our future and that we would need each other. Annie was not house trained, but she learned within a week. She was Dave's companion and often went to sleep on his lap. I fed her, took her out, walked her and taught her to run with me each morning.

When Annie was two years old, she was attacked by our neighbors' two-year-old German Shepherd. They had grown up together and played together in the past. But that day Annie did not want to play and Lizzy did. The German Shepherd took a big bite across Annie's shoulders and picked her up and shook her.

I tried to help but got knocked down. Dave ran toward us and beat the German Shepherd until she let go of Annie. At first the veterinarian thought it was just puncture wounds and stitched her up, but in the night Annie started bleeding. She had surgery the next day and for a month had three drains in her. It was a rough month, and I was her nurse, so our bond became even stronger as I nursed her back to health. She lived with the visible scars of her trauma. She was a survivor.

Then at three and a half years old, Annie lost her master, my husband, Dave died. Annie grieved the loss of her daily companion, and our bond grew stronger in our grief. Annie adapted easily to all the moves and changes. As long as I was with her, she was content. Annie enjoyed the counseling ministry at the Church because she received an abundance of attention and treats.

Annie and I had a good life together. She was always present in my loneliness. She heard my heart. She kept me active and engaged in life. As she aged and declined, she persevered, never giving up just changing how she lived life. She even accepted wearing diapers gracefully, and I gave her dignity by buying cute hot pink ones!

Why did Annie have to die at age eleven? I do not know. A better question is why did God give me Annie in the first place? What did I do to deserve her unconditional love and faithfulness? You will discover the reasons as you continue on this journey with me.

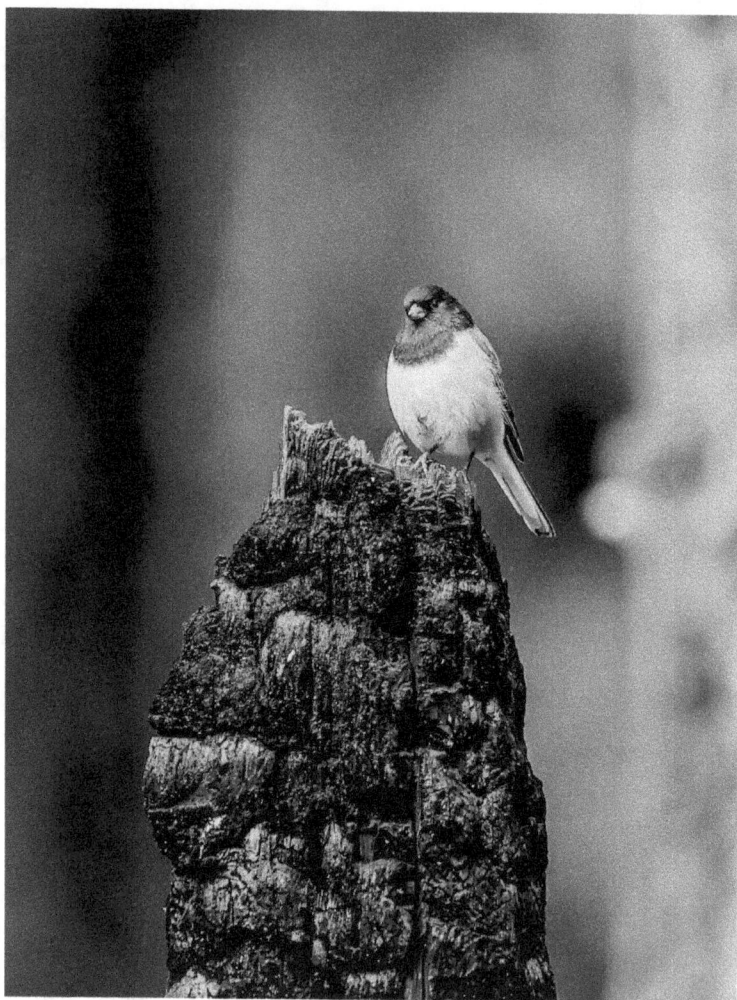

Chapter One

Trauma and Change

A nnie had experienced trauma in her life. She was born in a dog pound without the love of a family around her. She had been adopted but returned therefore she had the trauma of being abandoned by a family. She had the trauma of being a little dog among big dogs in a barn at the rescue group and had to defend herself. She had the trauma of being attacked. Then when she found her loving and forever family, her master died.

In the first three and a half years of her life, Annie experienced an intense amount of trauma, grief, and change that created anxiety within her. Since we adopted her, she had not been left alone only for short periods of time. We always returned, and she was never alone overnight. After Dave died, it was just Annie and me, and I had to navigate this journey of grief and still work and take care of Annie. I needed her and she needed me. I could not leave her alone all day, so I received permission to bring her to church with me. Annie began her life as a therapy dog. She was a natural. She had a new purpose. Annie loved all the attention from clients and anyone in the church building. Annie loved being petted and given treats from the church staff.

Annie would be with me all day at my office and then come home with me. I did not have to enter my house alone. She was beside me. We were companions. I talked with her, and she listened. She snuggled with me and licked my tears when I cried. Annie received all my feelings and frustrations. She never held anything against me but gave me unconditional love through the situations of our evolving life. She rescued me from the depth of my grief.

You, like Annie, have experienced trauma and change in life. You did not choose any of it, but still it has happened. Anxiety about the future fills your head. You worry. You feel alone, abandoned, and your primary person who helped you navigate these deep waters is gone. Life is not fair. True statement. But like, Annie, you keep persevering. The bond that God gave to Annie with me sustained her. She transferred to me her trust and security.

I have had to transfer to God my complete trust and security. While I have always trusted God, I had my husband with me who provided that sense of security that I did not have to do life alone. Then when Dave died, I transferred to Annie that sense of security so that I never felt alone. I experienced life with her. Now that Annie is with God and Dave in Heaven, my security and trust is in God alone. My foundation is stronger on which I stand because of Dave and Annie, my parents and Grandma, and all those who helped me build my foundation in Jesus. So I am not standing on a foundation I constructed by myself nor am I standing alone. All that love is still within me. I am stronger in Jesus because of loss and the influence of those who are now in Heaven.

People and dogs die, that is a part of life. Death is traumatic and changes our lives completely. God still can bring good out of all these difficult times when we put our trust in Him. Life changes but God is always the same and always with us. Trauma and loss do not need to define us and stop us from living. Annie is my example. Life did not start out easy for her, and it may not have started out good for you. Annie did not remain a victim but was rescued from it. God can rescue you too.

The victim role is an easy role to slip into after trauma. You have been the victim to grief and loss, and it has changed your life. You cannot change what has happened. You can only change how you deal with it. Will it consume you and define you and keep you stuck? Or will you accept it, release it, and take a step into change? It is your choice. You did not choose the change so do not feel guilty because you are choosing to live and find a new life.

To embrace is to accept willingly and enthusiastically. It is to grab hold of life and seize the life you have been given. No amount of wishing will bring back your past life. Embrace the change instead of fighting it. This is what you now have. This is now your life. You cannot live in the past. You have a new purpose and a new direction. Keep your eyes on Jesus. Begin to enjoy the journey. Your attitude will determine how you embrace life.

· · ● · ● · ● · · ·

Scripture

"We know that in everything God works for the good of those who love him. They are his people he called, because that was his plan." Romans 8:28 NCV

Step

Embrace Change

Pondering

Embrace the challenges and lean on Jesus. Jesus can take as much of the weight as you are willing to give to Him

Chapter Two

Dependence

Music has been central in my life and in my Christian walk. My mom played Gospel records on the stereo throughout my childhood. As a family, we attended Gospel Quartet concerts in all the area churches. As a teenager I preferred Christian music to Rock n' Roll. It filled my soul and prepared me to trust and depend on Jesus. Therefore, in my grief, music became part of the journey. It gave me an avenue to express my feelings when I could not put into words the emotions. One song by the Gospel group, The Perry's, became my song and my prayer in my grief – "Walk Me Through."

I listened to the songs with Annie beside me. She would lay her head on my lap and comfort me as we listened. The words and the music helped me to grieve and process my current situation. I was dependent upon Annie to be with me as I allowed the music to penetrate my soul.

Annie kept me going after my husband died. Her need to go outside and walk got me out of bed each day. She needed exercise so I kept running with her in the mornings and walking her at night. She would bring me her toys and want to play so she helped me focus somewhere else besides my grief. Annie needed to eat which reminded me to eat too. Annie gave me a good routine. I needed Annie, and we both needed each other to survive. Annie needed me to meet her basic needs of food, water, bodily function relief, and exercise. But she also needed me for reassurance. Her life kept changing, and she needed me to be her constant – her familiar person. I needed her to be that constant companion, too. We were dependent upon one another.

I did not want to admit this at first. I was independent and did not need anyone. I could do this alone. I was just being a responsible dog owner since she became my sole responsibility when Dave died. It did not take long before I accepted that I truly needed Annie. I was dependent on her. Annie taught me dependence is not bad. It matters though who you choose to depend on. Annie was faithful and never deviated from who she was and her dependence upon the one she trusted.

It was in the grief journey that Annie taught me total dependence upon God. Spell dog backward and you get God. God was working through Annie. I was learning that to be dependent is not a sign of weakness or wrong if you are dependent upon God. To depend on God is to rely upon, to count on, to lean on, rest upon. Annie relied on, counted on, leaned on and rested upon me. I needed to follow her example and depend upon God for everything. I was trusting God in all the "big stuff" and the "religious stuff", but not always the daily stuff and basics of life. I began to count on God always being with me through everything like Annie counted on me. Through Annie, I have learned and continue to grow dependent on God to hold my hand through every moment of every day. God will never leave me, and God accepts me as I am. He listens to my every need, feeling, frustration, and joy, and He keeps me grounded in Him.

Dependence upon God is the foundation for this different life. Society teaches us to focus on being independent and self-sufficient. Dependence is a weakness not a strength according to society. But in our faith, dependence means we cannot do life alone. God never intended for us to even try. God wants us to depend on His power, strength, and grace. With dependence comes the ability to take steps into this different life because it is God who leads, carries, holds, and directs us.

Dependence goes against the feelings within you. How do you depend on someone who did not answer the prayer for healing in the way desired? How do you depend on someone who allowed pain and suffering? How do you depend on someone who allows evil but who also allows freedom? This is difficult. You have a choice to depend on this Someone.

Dependence means I believe God is good. God is faithful. God loves me. God wants me to live fully the life He gave me. It is trusting God to guide my path not bless my selfish plans. It is believing God is not only the Creator of the Universe, but God is also personally with me. You cannot depend on Someone who is distant. God is present with you, and His presence is in you.

The steps I have taken through the last chapter of life have given me confidence I can make it through tough situations in life. On the outside it may seem I am strong and independent and can make decisions, but all of this is through my dependence on God. It is His strength, His guidance, and His love and grace that gives me the confidence to live this new and different life.

Dependence is relying not on my strength alone but on God's strength through me. I do not have to figure out the future; God is already there. I need to ask God to help me in living today. That is dependence.

· · • • · • • · · ·

Scripture

"Depend on the Lord; trust him, and he will take care of you." Psalm 37:5 NCV

Step

Depend on God

Pondering

When you are dependent on God and aware of His Presence, there you will find joy and abundant life and live in its fullness.

Chapter Three

Keep Going

Annie loved being outside and her beagle nose would follow the scent of any animal. Annie learned quickly to run with me each morning. At first, I held on to her leash and she ran beside me, but soon I dropped her leash and she would run behind me with her short leash dragging on the ground. She ran with me for almost nine years of her life.

I walked with Annie every day, too. She enjoyed walking in parks where she could be off her leash and go at her own pace. Annie would greet people on her walks. If I said "hi" to anyone, Annie assumed the person would want to pet her. When I lived in my hometown for a period of time after Dave died, I walked Annie every day in the neighborhood behind our home. One day, a gentleman was sitting on his porch, I waved and said "hi" which was Annie's signal to go up the driveway and meet him. Each day we walked, and he was on his porch, we went up the driveway to talk. Over time, we began a friendship with Vonice. He had graduated high school with my oldest brother. We talked about life and death, faith and fears and everything in between. When

Vonice died a year later, his wife, Regina, asked me to officiate at the funeral. The relationship had started with a walk and Annie.

Annie and I walked in every type of weather. It did not matter how hot or cold, if it was raining or snowing, and we even attempted to walk in the ice storm. Once we started, Annie was determined to finish. I became known as "Annie's mom" to most people we met on our walks. She would bark at other dogs to let them know she was in charge and that they did not scare her.

In my counseling, I have always encouraged clients to have some movement every day. It helps our mental and emotional health as well as our physical bodies. In this different life, Annie has taught me to stay as active as possible and to have some type of movement every day no matter how I feel. Annie was always eager to go for a walk. Walking helps to change the focus and give a different perspective on the day. Being in nature allows the focus to be more on creation and God's presence instead of getting lost in media or the daily drudge of life.

Some days Annie walked with purpose and direction, but other days she meandered back and forth smelling different rocks, trees, and grassy areas. The advantage Annie had was that I was with her and could direct her path even though some days she resisted my guidance. She still followed me.

Without having someone to lead us, we may get up in the morning determined to move and have a purpose for the day, but that all changes when we sit down. We scroll through the cell phone social media or turn on the TV. We get lost in the media drama and escape from living for hours. It becomes familiar, easy, and no effort is needed. We sit and our environment becomes unhealthy because of our lack of motivation. This is when depression can creep into daily living. No energy, no movement, and life piles up around us like dishes in a sink. The day is gone. We feel guilty about our lack of activity which adds to depression, but we do nothing to change it.

To keep from going down this dark hole in this different life you need to include some type of physical movement. It is stepping outside of your residence every day. It is moving around within your space. When the body remains idle, the thoughts become active and usually get stuck in the past. The familiar and comfortable is not always healthy. We meander without purpose and direction feeling lost at times. We go aimlessly from one thing to another not knowing what to do. We fear we may choose the wrong path, so we stop moving.

The past is completed. You cannot add to or take anything away from the past. You can walk in your memories in your mind, but you can no longer take up residence in the past. To live now is to keep moving forward into the current moment both physically and mentally.

Rest is essential. There was times Annie would sit down on a walk if I was talking with someone, but as soon as I said, "Let's go" she was ready. She rested but was alert and eager to keep going. Sometimes we need to rest, but remember it is just a rest not a completion. Annie needed me to lead her, or she would get lost or just stay where she was. We need God to guide us on this new and different path of life. God will keep whispering in our ear, "Keep going. I am right beside you all the way." Rest and reflection are necessary. Rest in God's presence. Allow God to help you process the next step. Keep walking forward into life.

· · · ● · ● · ● · ·

Scripture

"But the people who trust the Lord will become strong again. They will rise up as an eagle in the sky; they will run and not need rest; they will walk and not become tired." Isaiah 40:31 NCV

Step

Daily Movement

Pondering

Walk with Jesus in holy trust. When your mind is busy planning and worrying, you cannot hear the voice of God.

Chapter Four

Letting Go

I was Annie's person. She always needed to know where I was. She looked for me if I would walk away from her. She needed the assurance I was close by her side. I was her security. Most of the time Annie did what I said, but she also had a little stubborn streak in her. She had a mind and will of her own, but her loyalty was always to me.

Annie loved people who paid attention to her especially those who gave her belly rubs, played with her, and blessed her with dog treats. She always knew which clients brought her treats and was extra excited to see them. But if someone did not respond to her, she did not bother them. She left them alone to be who they were. She never forced herself onto anyone. It never bothered her. She would just lay down on her blanket, sigh, and go to sleep. If someone did not pay attention to her, it was their loss not hers.

People pleasing can be a struggle in life. Focusing so much on what others want to do and what they want you to be, that you lose yourself and become empty and exhausted. Annie taught me to let go of this familiar pattern of life. Why do something I do not like just because someone else wants me to do it. Nobody is in control of my life but me...and God. God is my person just like I was Annie's person. Letting go of other people's control and pleasing is a huge freedom.

This letting go defines a foundational piece of this different life. I do not need to live in the expectations of others. Sometimes I need to let others just be who they are and walk away like Annie to my own space – my own blanket – and just be me. It is a letting go of who we were in past relationships and past chapters of our lives. Yes, these parts and chapters are integrated into who you are, but you need not live in the expectations of others.

I had lost my way for a while. The path I knew was with Dave. It was familiar and when he died, Annie helped me stay on the path, but as I let go of the past, I wanted something more for my life. I went down a path for a time and lost my way and lost myself. I had to let go of trying to make things work my own way. I tried to re-create the familiar, but it was empty and not the same. I got lost in my own head but when I began to let go of my well worn path of familiarity, I found freedom in living outside the boundaries of my past and my thoughts. I let God be in my constant thoughts and when something got difficult, I knew God already knew about it and would carry me, His lost lamb, through it. I got lost on my own, but when I let go of me trying to figure it all out alone, God found me.

You have changed, and it is accepting being different and not expecting yourself to be and do and feel the same anymore. Annie quit running with me in the mornings when she was about nine years old. We went out to run one morning together, and when I looked for her next to me in the field, I could not find her. I looked toward the road, and there she was crossing the road by herself heading back to the house. The next day I took her again to run with me, and she did the same thing. I knew she was done running. I was sad, but I no longer expected her to be my running partner. It did not change my love for her or who she was. She just walked in the evenings with me.

Letting go means you do not live in the past. You remember it because it is integrated into who you are now. You have to stop trying to recreate the past; it cannot be done. You have to let go of the pain and hurt of the past; it only makes it harder to move on. It was real. It was wrong. You cannot change it. You can learn from it. Let go of the negative voices in your head. Listen to how Jesus sees you – loved, forgiven, and a new creation in Him.

Letting go of expectations frees you to live in today and begin accepting who you are now. It is letting go of trying to be perfect – only God is perfect. Live in God's perfection and stop striving to be someone you will never become. Let go of trying to be what you imagine others want you to be and begin finding who you are now. Letting go of who you once were because life has changed and altered your planned life, and you must move on. Let go of worrying about the future and begin living in the present. Let go and let God take control.

• • • • • • • • • •

Scripture

"Forgetting the past and straining toward what is ahead, I keep trying to reach the goal and get the prize for which God called me through Christ to the life above." Philippians 3:13-14 NCV

Step

Let go and Let God

Pondering

You are meant to go through your troubles and hurts only once. Do not keep reliving them and reviewing them in your mind. Do not live in the past.

Chapter Five

Boundaries

Annie was usually on a leash when we walked. At times, I would let her go free in the yard, and she abided by her limits except when her nose took charge. Her beagle nose would pick up the scent of an animal and off she would run. I could yell and tell her to stop, but when her nose took control, her ears shut down. I would have to run after her and soon she would stop and roll over when I got to her, she knew she had crossed her boundaries. When I counseled at the church her boundary was my office. Sometimes she would sit with her nose out the door, but her body was in the office. Other times, her craving for a dog treat would get her in trouble. She would run from my office to the church office to get a treat from Val who worked in the office.

Boundaries kept Annie safe and protected, but at times they were difficult to keep even for a dog. Boundaries are healthy for dogs and for people as well. They are more than property lines or personal space in a home. Boundaries are limits set in relationships, too. They involve emotional closeness and control.

They are set for protection. Boundaries also define your personal responsibility in a relationship.

To live this different life, boundaries are needed in relationships. It is setting limits on allowing others to be in control of your life. It is recognizing not everyone who used to be in your life is healthy for you now. You have changed. Sometimes you still need to interact with people who are controlling and unhealthy. This is where the box concept is needed. Imagine that person lives in a box. It has a door where you enter and interact with the person in the box, but you do not try to change or fix the box. The box also has an exit door. You can leave the person in the box and go live your own life outside the box. You just set a healthy boundary for yourself with this box concept.

Boundaries are essential for yourself, too. It is setting a boundary from living in your past sin, guilt, regret, pain, hurt or whatever holds you back. It is forgiving yourself and not going back there.

The past is concluded. You cannot change it. Set the boundary of completion. Outline your space and define who you are.

Set a boundary with anxiety and worry. You were not created to be anxious nor worry all the time about the future and all the details of life. God created you to trust Him. Your personality is not being a worrier or an anxious person. Life has influenced you. Set a boundary and begin living in the present and focusing on what is in front of you. Put events on the calendar but do not focus on the details until you get there. God is already in the future. Leave the future in God's hands. God created humanity to live in the boundary of one twenty-four-hour period of time. God protects humanity from the weight of too much time. God created you to live in the boundary of today.

Set a boundary on negativity and being a victim. Bad things happened and I am sorry for the bad that has happened in your life. You did not deserve it, but it does not need to define you either. Learn from it. Name it so it does not have control over you anymore. Leave it in your past and set a boundary not to go there anymore.

Set a boundary in living in a performance-based relationship with God. You do not need to earn God's favor or acceptance. You will never be good enough on your own. God is good and through His grace, we are good. God loves you and gives you grace and mercy as a free gift. With God, boundaries of obedience are essential to growth and staying within the will and protection of God.

Set a boundary on what you put in your thoughts and in your mind. Set a boundary to the things of this world that pull you away from God.

"Capture every thought and make it give up and obey Christ." 2 Corinthians 10:5 NCV

Choose to listen to what will build you up and help you grow in God's favor and grace. Set a boundary on profanity and words that degrade and hurt others and yourself. Whatever you put into your body and mind controls you. Set a boundary to social media, any media that separates you from God's love and does not glorify God. These need to be avoided.

Set a boundary to what is acceptable behavior and what is healthy for you to experience. You get to choose where you go, who you interact with, what you watch and listen to. If it does not build you up, glorify God, bring you joy, or assist in your growth, then set a boundary.

The boundaries are for your benefit to protect you sometimes even from yourself. Begin to define who you are in Jesus and use your relationship with Jesus to set healthy boundaries for your life. The Holy Spirit is given to guide you in each moment of life.

· · · ● · ● · · ·

Scripture

Moses said to the Lord, "The people cannot come up Mount Sinai, because you yourself warned us, 'Put limits around the mountain and set it apart as holy.'"   *Exodus 19:23 NIV*

Step

Define your space and set limits.

Pondering

Live within the boundaries of today.

Chapter Six

Release

Annie was a wonderful listener regarding hearing my feelings and frustrations especially in the last seven years of her life. She listened in counseling sessions with clients and provided comfort and compassion by her presence. Annie kept secrets, and I could talk to her about everything that I kept inside of me. I released all the emotions that were within me through running with Annie and talking with Annie and God. Keeping feelings bottled up inside is not healthy. Emotionally releasing them allows you to name them and free yourself from the burden and damage that can happen when they consume and build up inside.

I have had to now release Annie to Heaven. She has completed her life on earth. She is released from the suffering and pain of her earthly body. Just like all those I have loved, Annie is free from the burden of this earth and dwells in peace in Heaven. She completed her purpose. To be released is to be set free from the confinement of this earthly dwelling. It takes time to release living constantly in the past memories and feelings of loss and emptiness. Release is not forgetting because I will always remember Annie and the joy of her in my life.

You have had to release someone you loved to Heaven, and to now release yourself from existing only in the past. It is releasing yourself from the guilt that your life continues on earth, but your loved one's life is completed. Remember, your loved ones are living in Heaven. Release them to live there and allow their influence and love to be your stepping stone onto this different path of life. If you do not release, you stay stuck and just exist in trying to maintain a past that is gone.

Releasing Annie to Heaven has been a process for me. I held her as she died. I carried her body to the funeral home to be cremated. I washed all her bedding and donated it to the shelter. I gave most of her toys and food to someone who just adopted a dog. I released her belongings to those who could use them, so her legacy continues. I kept her prayer blanket and 2 favorite toys and leash. Her leash still hangs on a hook beside the door. She is present with me in spirit. I buried her ashes beside my parents. Release is not clearing our loved one completely from our life but repositioning them so as to take steps into the life that is now before us.

This release is a freedom to live again and maybe even love again. The release is to be set free from the confinement of just existing. When I would release Annie from the confinement of her leash and set her free, she would run in circles, roll, and enjoy her freedom to go wherever she wanted without the pull of the leash holding her back. Annie enjoyed the moment. When you release yourself to begin living, you focus on moments, too. Find joy in a moment – the sunrise, the sound of the rain, the smile of a child, the taste of your favorite dessert. You allow the moment to absorb into your soul. After Annie would run in her freedom, she would just lay in the grass or mulch and just rest in her freedom.

Release is a letting go of how life used to be – a release of trying to re-create the past in your present life. No matter how hard you try, it will always leave you empty. It is also releasing of the past in other people's lives. They are not the same person either. It is releasing people to be who they are. Sometimes it is also releasing people who were a vital part of your past but who now have completed their journey with you. Your paths have reached a crossroad and go in different directions. Give thanks for them and close the chapter on your relationship with them.

Release also involves control. It is releasing – letting go of – the need to control every aspect of your life or the lives of those around you. You do not want to feel the hurt and pain of loss again, so you attempt to control everything and everyone around you. Annie had a little rebellion in her especially when I tried to control where she laid down by putting her blanket where I wanted her to be. Sometimes she would move to a rug, move her blanket, or lay down beside the door instead. I had to let her just be where she was comfortable. It is releasing control and giving it to God. Releasing all people and situations to God. Easier said than done. This is a process but a necessary step to live in this different life. God is in control. Freedom is found in this releasing!

• • • • • • • • • •

Scripture

"The Lord God has put his Spirit in me, because the Lord has appointed me to tell the good news to the poor. He has sent me to comfort those whose hearts are broken, to tell the captives they are free, and to tell the prisoners they are released."   Isaiah 61:1 NCV

Step

Feel the Freedom in Releasing

Pondering

You may think holding on makes you strong but releasing gives you freedom and peace when you release to God.

Chapter Seven

Trust

Annie trusted me. She trusted I would take care of her basic needs of food, water, shelter, going outside, and attention. She trusted I would protect her and provide for her. She trusted I would return from an errand or a trip and come back to her. It was always difficult for me to leave her in the care of a friend or family member. I knew Annie wanted to always be with me, and I knew she would be taken care of when I left her with friends or family. Annie did not know how long I would be gone, but I believe she trusted I would return. I always told her I would be back and because I always came back, I believe she trusted me. I also trusted Annie to always be excited to see me and to give me unconditional love. She never held it against me that I left her for a period of time. She always loved me and wanted to be with me. We were bound together in trust and love.

Trust is a firm belief, an acceptance, a confidence, a certainty. To trust is to take a risk and accept what you believe is actually true. In order to move into this new life, trust needs to be part of the firm foundation. The uncertainty of life shakes the core of your being.

You have walked through your world being turned upside down. As you look back, I hope you recognize you have survived because God has held your hand and sometimes carried you. God has been faithful. God is faithful. God will always be faithful. Even when you cannot see God or feel His presence, God is still with you. You trusted God even when you were in the darkness of grief. You may not have named it trust but you held on. You must trust Him more as you continue living forward.

It is storing up trust in God when life is good so when you go through tough times, you remember the times God has been faithful and you keep trusting God's faithfulness. Your trust is in your foundation. Just like Annie trusted me because I had never let her down and always came back to her, you build trust in God when you recognize God has walked you through some really tough situations. God has always been with you and always will.

As I live in this different life, Annie has helped me trust God even more. Annie trusted I would always provide for her even when she did not see me. I am trusting God in what I cannot see – the future. Instead of planning everything and trying to control the future, I am trusting God and relaxing in God's presence. I trust God will lead me especially, when I surrender to Him. I am trusting God in each situation and believing God is with me even if I do not see or feel His Presence. Trust is faith.

You experience peace when you let go of trying to control or fix every situation on your own. When you attempt to control and fix everything around you, this raises your anxiety and worry and erases all trust. You think your future is all on your shoulders to figure out. This is overwhelming and exhausting. You do not even trust yourself enough to accomplish all that needs to be done. Trust and peace go hand in hand. Peace comes by trusting that God is in control and is your constant companion. Peace is trusting the future to God and living in the present in God's presence. Trust is reaching out in the darkness of this different life and believing God is right there with you.

I am trusting myself more because I know God is with me every moment of every day. Annie's constant companionship gave me such comfort during the tough days of my journey. She taught me that relying on another is not weakness but a strength when you surrender to the love and support of another. Through Annie's trust and dependence on me, I have learned to trust and depend daily – each moment – on God. This different life is built on the foundation of trust in God. I do not need to know the next step; I just need to trust that God will take the step with me. Annie knew I was with her each step of her life even her last step, and I know God is with me each step. I just need to live in the present and not worry about the future steps. God is already there. There is peace in trusting the Lord. When someone or something comes to mind, ask God if it is part of His plan for you today. If not, wait for God's timing. Trust.

· · · ● · ● · ● · ·

Scripture

"Trust the Lord with all your heart, and don't depend on your own understanding." Proverbs 3:5 NCV

Step

Trust God. Accept yourself as you are.

Pondering

Worry is a form of rebellion – doubting God will take care of you and the situation.

Chapter Eight

Adventure

Annie was my traveling partner from the first day I adopted her. Her first ride was on my lap, wrapped in a blanket at six months old. She licked my face as to say, "Thank you." She curled up and fell asleep on the drive to her new home. Annie never got car sick and was always excited to jump into the vehicle with me. The back seat of each vehicle I have owned was her space with a dog cover and blanket. Her nose prints were always on the windows. It did not matter where we were going, she loved to travel. Annie just wanted to be with me. The only place she did not like going was to the Vet, and she figured out quickly each Veterinarian's Office.

Annie had quite the extensive travel experience – Lewes in Delaware, Gettysburg, Outer Banks, Niagara Falls, Vermont, and all over Ohio. Sometimes she lived in the backseat when I needed to take her with me because she was not allowed in the place I was going. She attended many seminars and enjoyed the ride and the attention she received at the end.

When she was in the backseat sometimes she would whimper and needed me to touch her for reassurance. I would reach back and stroke her for a short time and then she would settle down and sleep. She trusted me as the driver. Annie was always open to a new adventure. It was a joy to see her jump out of the backseat, begin to smell the area and figure out if she had been there before. If not, she wanted to explore and make sure it was safe for me. Usually, if it was a familiar place she liked, she sensed it before we arrived. She would sit up, look out the window and get all excited. She knew the joy of this trip and who would be there to greet her.

Annie's last trip was her goodbye. She snuggled in my arms with her blanket around her as we headed to the Vet's office. Our hearts touched and beat together. She licked my face as if to say, "Thank you" for the last time.

Annie taught me the joy of travel and adventure. She did not need to know where she was going, but she was always willing to go because she would be with me. In this different life, be open to new adventures. You do not need to know how it will turn out – that is anxiety creeping into your head. I enjoy just getting into the vehicle and choosing a direction and just taking off for an adventure that day. It is an adventure to experience wherever you end up for that day. These have been some of my favorite trips because not knowing where you are going can make the trip more exciting and adventuresome.

Experience and try out new adventures. You will not know until you try if it is what you like. Just because you do it once, does not mean it becomes something you will do again. Like horseback riding in the mountains of Maui – glad I did it, but it is not something I will do again. One and done. Great adventure.

An adventure is an exciting, unusual, not familiar activity. It is going into the unknown which can cause fear and anxiety. Remember, you are trusting God as you move into this new life. It is not going on the same trips or going to the same places you did in your former life. It will be too close to the same and cause emptiness. If you are going to the same places with someone else it may feel uncomfortable, and you want the memory to stay as it was in the past. So try new places – different restaurants, parks, places of interest, and even with different people. It is finding with whom you are comfortable and with whom can you just be yourself and not have to take care of them or have them control the adventure.

Be open to allowing new experiences and people in your life. It may feel like you have no clue what to do or where you are going, and you are probably right – you don't. Let God be the driver in this new book of your life. Ask God for direction and trust Him. Do not ask people for directions who have not yet traveled this road that you have been on for a while. They have not yet experienced the loss and their whole world being turned upside down. You are trying to figure out how to live and how to find out who you are and what you like and where life will take you now. They are still living in the familiar without the changes you have experienced.

Adventure is also part of changing your thinking and view of life. Life is not what you planned, but as you move into this different, it is changing your attitude and view of life. Life can still be good if you take the risk of actually trying new experiences. Try. God is holding your hand. Trust Him. Let's go!

· · · ●·●●·· ·

Scripture

"Direct me in the path of your command, for there I find delight."
Psalm 119:35 NIV

Step

Try New Experiences

Pondering

Give yourself fully to the adventure of today. Walk boldly into the day holding God's hand.

Chapter Nine

Foundation

The beginning of Annie's life was unstable and sad. Being born in a dog pound she had no family of her own, no comforts, minimal food, and no space to call her own. She was adopted and then returned so she had no sense of worth or security. When we adopted her, we had to create a new beginning for her that was healthy and would allow her to grow and develop into the dog God created her to be. We gave her love, security, her own home, people who would never leave her and the assurance her needs would always be met.

Annie's life confirms that even when our foundation – the beginning of our lives – is not sturdy or healthy, it can be rebuilt. Where you began life may influence and be a point of departure for your journey, but you need not remain stuck in it. Some of Annie's need to be touched and her anxiety of being left came from her early days in the dog pound. It influenced but did not define the essence of her life.

The foundation is the groundwork for how life is lived. The foundation gives the shape to one's life. It includes values, principles, perspectives, basic rudiments, and the essence of the person. The foundation, if not built on lasting and sturdy ingredients will cause whatever is built upon it to sink or not hold the weight. Foundational stones include faith, love, trust, purpose, service.

Your foundation becomes stronger throughout the experiences of life. You test the strength of your foundation through the trials and hurts of life. Not the way you want it to happen, but it is when you find the places that are crumbling and need repairs. You rely on the foundation to hold you up and not let you sink. Jesus is the cornerstone of your foundation. He holds your life together. All those you have loved and have guided you in life, their love and influence, also firms up your foundation.

Sometimes what you put in your foundation is distorted and not really who you want to be or who you were created to be. Just like Annie, she thought she was abandoned and unwanted, but only for the first six months of her life. We rebuilt her life with our love and security. I believe her need to be touched came from her past and lack of human contact. Annie grew into who she was created to be when love, trust, security and acceptance was added to the foundation of her life.

As you grow into this different life, you have to examine your own foundation and name the stones you have built your life upon. It is not starting over but firming up your foundation or uncovering it. You may have to rediscover the basic principles of your life. Sometimes daily living and the views of the world get in the way of what you believe is important and essential to life. You may have just been existing and life became mundane and just functional. You lost purpose and meaning. Now is the time to dust off the foundational stones and shore them up. Fill in the holes. Remind yourself what you value and believe.

It is taking an assessment of your life as you live into this new adventure. What do you believe? Where is God in your foundation? Are you building your life on Jesus or the world or someone else's view? It is now you. Yes, others have influenced you, but it is now the time to commit to your own values, beliefs, and view of life. Take it all in from your past. Sort it out. Take a stand. Name the stones of your foundation.

• • • • • • • • • •

Scripture

"The foundation that has already been laid is Jesus Christ, and no one can lay down any other foundation." *I Corinthians 3:11 NCV*

Step

Build on Your Groundwork

Pondering

Even though you mess up, keep pressing on. Learn from your mistakes. Trust your foundation in Jesus.

Chapter Ten

Recognize Your Needs

After Dave died, Annie and I needed each other for support and companionship. Neither of us wanted to be alone so we were together as much as possible. Annie has always needed to be touched and given the assurance someone cared and was with her. She would whimper or use her paw to touch me when she was not receiving the attention she wanted. She laid beside my chair on her blanket when I counseled. Most days she needed me to touch her until she fell asleep. Annie always needed reassurance. Annie's basic physical needs of food, water, shelter, sleep, walks were met every day of our lives together. Her desire to be touched was constant so sometimes I had to tell her, "Not now" or "That's enough." She would just sigh and lay down a short distance from me. She wanted me to know her need was not being met and she was not pleased. Touch is a basic need.

Needs and wants. My basic needs, like Annie's, are always met. I always have had air, food, clothing, water, sanitation, shelter, the ability to have movement. I may have wanted something different or more, but my basic physical needs have always been satisfied. Annie also fulfilled part of my need for touch after Dave died. Touch is an emotional and physical need that states someone cares and is present. Another emotional need is that life needs meaning and purpose. Annie found purpose to her life by being my personal emotional support companion and a therapy dog to my clients.

You need meaning and purpose to live in this different life. It may not be the same purpose as in the past. Purpose creates hope and fulfillment – a reason to live and contribute to life. Purpose is found in God. It is glorifying God in who you are and all you do. It does not mean having some huge profound purpose that changes the world. It is finding meaning in each day – being present with God and thanking Him. It is expressing compassion and care to a stranger or friend. It is simply being available to be used by God to make a difference. I find purpose and meaning in each day by asking God, "Who do you want me to connect with today?"

I had to let go of wanting my old life back early in my loss. I did not want to let it go and tried to keep everything familiar, but it just brought emptiness. I could not recreate it. I needed to find a new way of living. I needed to accept my life had changed and I needed to change with it. I was different. The people around me stayed the same, living like nothing had turned their world upside down. While they were sad about the loss, it did not change their day-to-day life like mine. I needed to figure out life again.

A basic emotional need is relationships – the need to be connected. God created people to be in relationship with one another. Annie's connectional need was met in me. She met part of my need for a time. My work and counseling kept me connected to people, but I no longer had my primary person to live life with. Annie could not help make decisions or carry the load of daily tasks. I have come to see this need for a primary person relationship fulfilled as I move closer to Jesus. While I have always had a personal relationship with Jesus, giving my heart and life to Jesus when I was in seventh grade, my dependence on His presence has grown. I hold His hand and He walks me through each situation and day. God sits with me, and I am trying to be aware of His constant and abiding presence.

While I need people in my life and enjoy my friendships, I need to choose who I want to step closer to and who I want to complete my time together. I need to choose my boundaries with others.

I pull some closer and step farther away from others. You have a need to be connected. You want people to care and like you, but they cannot define or control you.

You need to take care of yourself. Make yourself a priority. That is not selfish. God created you as His child and you are wonderfully made. You need to be who God created you to be. You need to choose to be yourself. Recognize in this new life, your basic need is to find who you are now.

• • • ● • ● • • •

Scripture

"God chose you to be his people, so I urge you now to live the life to which God called you. Always be humble, gentle, and patient, accepting each other in love." Ephesians 4:1-2 NCV

Step

Be Kind to Yourself

Pondering

God leads you to be who He created you to be not what the world wants you to be.

Chapter Eleven

What Do You Like?

A nnie loved belly rubs. She would let anyone pet her and as she got comfortable with them, she would roll over and want her belly rubbed. Sometimes she would then fall asleep. She loved having her ears rubbed and being petted, but the belly rub was her favorite. Annie loved treats. Her favorites were cucumbers, watermelon, hot dogs, and any dog treat Val would give her at the church office. Val was the treat lady to Annie and along with a treat came a belly rub, too. Annie ate cucumbers after she greeted each client. She would then bark for her treat. Annie knew what she liked. She would sniff something before she ate it, and if it did not smell good to her, she walked away.

In the past you may have chosen what you ate based on someone else's preferences. You went to restaurants someone else liked and participated in activities because someone else enjoyed them. Now that it is just you, what do you like? You have had to maneuver the grocery store as your first reality in choosing for yourself. That was difficult for me because I always bought what Dave liked. After Dave's death, I just chose food for each meal and ate that same thing for months. Overtime, I have figured out what I like and do not like. I have gained confidence in choosing for me not because someone else likes it. Big step because I made myself a priority. Having a preference is not disrespectful to anyone else. It is just admitting to yourself that you matter and can have an opinion and a preference.

When I defined my food preferences, it gave me confidence to define other choices in life. I gave myself permission to make choices others did not agree with, but what I liked. I was becoming my own person in all areas of life. I made choices of where I went, what I did, and with whom I spent time. When I could choose tangible things, then it became easier to make emotional and internal decisions for my life. It was my life not anybody else's life. I recognized that some of the things I did in the past were done because of my husband and my choosing not to do them anymore did not take anything away from our life together. It was time to do it for me.

To live different, you first need to figure out who you are – what you like, what you enjoy and how you want to spend your resources and time. I found I loved to travel and especially liked flying to destinations. I enjoy the beach, the sunshine, bike riding, hiking and walking, writing, visiting friends and especially my elderly friends. I do not like watching TV, especially sports, and I like being active. I like exploring little towns and being in nature. Big cities are not for me. I share a few of my discoveries so that you begin to figure out who you are and what you like. It is up to you.

I loved Annie, but now I like the freedom that comes from not being responsible for a dog. Try out your new life. The experiences of your past are always a part of your foundation, but you do not need to keep doing those same things. They were part of your past and you cannot re-create them. It will never feel the same. Because you are different because of the loss and change, what you experience now in life needs to be different. You can keep some of the same things if you truly enjoy them. If you do something and do not like it, chalk it up as an experience and move on. Now you have learned what you do and do not like. Keep trying new things. Take the risk. Experience life. Someone will always tell you not to do it or question why you are doing what you are doing. Most of the time people say this because they are afraid to risk and try something new. You can do anything even if you are afraid. Remember, God is holding your hand as you experience life.

Everywhere you go, you take yourself with you. Start enjoying your own company. Start taking opportunities to live in the moments that stand before you. Accept yourself for who you are. Give yourself permission to step into life one step at a time. Forgive yourself. Love who you are and who you are becoming. You cannot change the past or live in the past anymore. It has helped to define you. You get a choice of who you are now in the present and who you will be in the future. Choose to step into this future.

· · · ● · ● ● · · ·

Scripture

"Each person should judge his own actions and not compare himself with others. Then he can be proud for what he himself has done. Each person must be responsible for himself." Galatians 6:4-5 NCV

Step

Step Into Who You are Becoming

Pondering

God loves me for who I am, not for what I do.

Chapter Twelve

Dealing With Disappointments

When Annie wanted something and I told her to either "wait" or "not now," she would bark back at me like she was talking back to me. I am glad I could not understand what she was barking. Annie had some stubbornness in her, and we would be at a standstill with each other. But most of the time, she would just sigh and lay down and wait. The times I would have to leave her home alone, I would take her outside to do her business, and she would stop by my vehicle on the way inside. I would tell her that she could not go with me this time. She would put her head down, go inside and go lay on her blanket or in her bed. She was sad and disappointed I was leaving her alone. It made me feel like a bad person, but she was always excited to see me when I returned. Just as I could not always please Annie, you have to accept that you cannot always please others.

Disappointments happen. You are displeased that life has turned out this way and you have to begin a new life you did not choose. It is discouraging to know what you planned and hoped for will not happen. Discontentment fills the day, and you feel frustrated with the circumstances of life. Regret seeps into your life as life was not fulfilled to your desired expectations. This is now your life. You can feel sorry for yourself or accept it and figure out the next steps toward living this different life.

Even when you accept this new life, disappointments continue to occur. You are disappointed in other people and how they have moved on even after promising that nothing would change. You are disappointed in yourself. It seems every time you take steps and try something new, it does not work out the way you expected. In the past when this happened after Dave died, I still had Annie to vent my frustrations of life. Now she is gone.

Disappointments happen in all areas of life. I am learning to find ways to accept that God has a different plan than mine. There is a purpose in the change and something I need to learn through the disappointment. Sometimes, it is that you need to allow God to be in control and surrender to His guidance. You would not do this if everything worked out like you planned. You would rely on yourself not God. Sometimes, God wants you to rest instead of being so busy so He slows you down. Sometimes, you just need to recognize that it is OK to not have it all together – nobody does no matter how much someone tries to pretend.

I am learning to release to God how I feel when something goes wrong. Even in the daily things of life. The other night, I took my last jar of honey out of the cabinet. I turned quickly and hit the jar against the counter top and the glass jar broke. I was not paying attention to what I was doing but thinking of what I was going to do next. The jar and honey went all over the kitchen floor. I was frustrated. I lost all the honey and had to clean up the broken glass and honey. It was a sticky mess that took time to clean up. I was disappointed in myself for doing something so stupid even though it was an accident. I knew I was dealing with disappointments differently because I was calm. I took a deep breath and sighed and prayed, "OK God, let's clean up this mess together. We got it."

I am also learning to not allow one disappointment to ruin the whole day. It is saying, "OK, that did not work, I will try something else or go in a different direction." It is not putting together everything that goes wrong and living in "woe is me" mode. It is letting go and moving on. It is letting things roll off instead of absorbing them. It is finding positives even amid the disappointment. It is recognizing the loss but also looking at what is still around you and the memories and love that will always remain in your heart. It is finding things to be thankful for. Not everything in life can be fixed, healed, or made perfect. Life is living in the middle of the imperfections, disappointments and finding joy and contentment.

• • • ● • ● • • • •

Scripture

"People make plans in their minds, but the Lord decides what they will do." Proverbs 19:9 NCV

Step

Find a Balance in Your Life

Pondering

Time. Space. Grace.

Chapter Thirteen

Live In Front of You

Annie enjoyed whatever life gave her that was in front of her. If her toy moose was there, she played with it. If a water bottle was given to her, she would unscrew the cap and take off the plastic ring. If her food was in front of her, she ate it. She enjoyed the client who was in front of her. When she jumped out of the backseat of my vehicle, it did not matter to her where she was, she enjoyed the adventure. She was not picky about life. Whatever was in front of her, she enjoyed.

All I have is today – what is right in front of me. In this different life, I am learning to stay present – to be present with God and to live fully in the day. When I am with someone, I stay in the moment with them and not focus on what comes next. I try to be fully attentive to the person who is in front of me.

Every time I begin to think and worry about a future event, I reach out and take God's hand and pray, "God, pull me back into this moment." Anxiety is usually a worry about the future, what might happen and being anxious about all the possible problems. There is nothing wrong with planning and preparing when it comes to certain commitments. I need to prepare when I give talks, officiate at funerals and weddings, take a trip, but I do not need to live in this future event. I put it on my calendar, do the necessary preparations and then release it to God. God is already in the future, and I need to remain fully in the present. Worry and anxiety is a fruitless effort to control the future. I have no control over the future. Prepare and release the rest into God's hands.

Sometimes the focus of anxiety is on the past, and I get lost in my head reliving the past. I feel regret of what I did wrong or what I could have done differently. I live in the regret. I cannot change it. The past is filled with a mixture of memories. I am trying to celebrate the good ones and forgive myself and others for the hurt and sin.

Live in front of you. If you do not like what is in front of you then change it. Change your environment, your space, your location, your possessions, your clothes, your image. The relationships around you may be negative and not fulfilling then put boundaries around them and seek healthy connections. So many times the reason for not living in the present is that the present is not healthy. Change it.

Fully means completely to the farthest extent without reservation or hesitation. Present is to be where your feet are and to focus on the now. Not only are you physically present in the now, but your thoughts are right in front of you without any anxiety or thought of what will happen next. Can you be fully present?

Life has taught me to be fully present. Yes, I make plans and schedule clients and events, but I am learning to enjoy what is in front of me. To slow down and not have to be busy planning the next event or way to live out God's calling on my life. I have spent most of my ministry trying to find ways of being active for God and how much could I accomplish for God each week. Activity felt like I was fulfilling what God wanted for me.

Now in this different life, I pray each day for God's Spirit to fill me with His power and strength and lead me to what I am to do to glorify God. Some days it is to praise God and rest in the beauty of creation and God's presence. Some days it is to take the hand of Jesus and walk with someone else on the journey. Some days it is just to be – to be in the feelings and emotions of the journey, to be present and take the next step, to just be.

· • • ● • ● ● • • ·

Scripture

Jesus said, "I came to give life – life in all its fullness." John 10:10 NCV

Step

Be Fully Present in the Now

Pondering

When you are in the moment both mentally and physically, you have acquired the art of living.

Chapter Fourteen

Focused Surrender

Annie's main focus in life was to enjoy life and to be with me. She loved to run, play, sleep, eat, be in the sunshine, and interact with people. When she stayed focused on these enjoyable parts of life, she was the perfect dog. When Annie stayed focused on pleasing me and being with me, we were both happy and content. When I got distracted and did not keep an eye on her, that is when she got into trouble. Annie had a strong stubborn will and it would take over at times, then she would lose her primary focus. Her beagle nose would take charge and her focus became whatever scent she caught. She would run after the animal her nose smelled.

When Annie finally stopped running, and she heard me or saw me running after her, she would roll over and surrender to me. Once I talked to her and told her that was not what I expected out of her, she would lick my face as if to say, "I'm sorry." I could not be mad at her for doing what was instinctive to a beagle dog. She knew it was not what I wanted her to do so she would surrender and focus back on being with me.

Where is your focus? In the past, you may have focused on the needs of a spouse, your family, and the workload of your job or home. Other people took priority and your attention. You tried to meet the needs and expectations of those around you and make their lives better. Sometimes that can leave you empty and exhausted. Been there. Done that, too.

I have learned, like Annie, to surrender to my Master. To surrender each day and every part of me to God. Oh, this is a process and I have to surrender control throughout the day. I take it back from God. To surrender to God is to believe God knows what is best better than I do for myself. I am learning to trust that God's will and desire for my life can be trusted. To surrender to God is to see each day as a clean slate for God to fill not me.

I am learning to focus more on God each and every day. To rest in God's presence. To just be with God and not be focused on tasks and accomplishments that I think will earn favor with God. It is being aware of God in every part of life. To see God in the beauty around me. When your focus is on the world and the tasks of life, you become overwhelmed, negative, filled with anxiety and worry, and you make choices that are not healthy. You may feel like running away from the one who cares for you the most just like Annie would run from me.

It is yielding to God as the authority of your life. Annie relented to my guidance for her life, but her strong will would cross the boundaries at times. She would make sure I knew she had a will of her own. When she took her eyes off of me, she could get lost, hurt, or allow the things around her to lead her off the path away from me. When I lose focus on God, the things of this world take control and lead me down paths away from the One who loves and cares for me the most. I need to come back to God and surrender again and again.

In this different life, my desire is for God to be my main influence not the distractions of this world. When I focus more on God, anxiety and worry releases their hold on my thoughts. I know God loves me and cares for me and wants to guide me. I am increasing my attention daily to God's presence. My focus in life is pleasing and glorifying God.

You and I have lived our lives so focused on caring and fixing situations for others that we have forgotten ourselves. It is time to change the focus of life. God is the one who cares and loves us unconditionally. Surrendering to God is saying to God, "I am exhausted and tired of going in circles and feeling like nothing has changed. I want you to lead me and change my focus of life."

• • • ●•●• • •

Scripture

Jesus said, "Come to me, all of you who are tired and have heavy loads, and I will give you rest. Accept my teachings and learn from me, because I am gentle and humble in spirit, and you will find rest for your lives." Matthew 11:28-29 NCV

Step

Rest in God's Presence

Pondering

Stillness before God accomplishes more than busyness. Be still and cease striving to be enough. You are enough in God's eyes.

Prayer of Surrender

God, I am a sinner. I confess my sins to you. I accept Jesus Christ as my Savior and Lord. I surrender my life to You and Your will for my life. Amen.

Chapter Fifteen

Joy and Laughter

A nnie could always make me laugh with her antics, her dog smile, or just how she looked at me and turned her head as if she actually understood me. I could get her so excited that she would run in circles and then stop quickly, put her chin on the ground, and her rear in the air. If I jumped toward her, she would jump up and start running in circles again. She would repeat this several times and then just crash and roll over on her side. When Annie finished eating, she used her blanket as her napkin. First, Annie would roll her face on the blanket as if she were cleaning it. Then she would use her nose to get under it, throw it up and wrap herself in the blanket. She could make me laugh just when I needed it. Annie remained puppy-like all her life.

Laughter is good medicine for the soul and the body. Laughter enhances your oxygen intake, stimulates your heart and lungs, and releases endorphins in your brain which make you feel better. Laughter also helps you not to take yourself so seriously. It reminds you to enjoy life. Laughter does not disregard the pain and hurt of life, but that joy can exist with it. Laughter brings healing to the hurt soul.

A child lives for the moment and finds joy in the simplest of things like the box instead of the gift inside it, pots and pans instead of the expensive toys, and will giggle just to hear themselves make noise. As adults, you tend to think you have to act mature and lose the childlike gifts of joy. You have journeyed through the sadness, loss, pain and hurt, and you will experience it again. You need to give yourself permission to experience joy and laughter again. Yes, for moments but also to live joy – an inner contentment of life. This is the life you now have. Nothing brings back the past and nothing takes away from your previous life. It is completed. To live in this different life, joy needs to be central. It is a childlike joy that is given by God, your Father, to His children.

Try it. Jump in the puddles and walk in the rain. Eat the ice cream with sprinkles. Play checkers. Have a tea party. Be silly. Find happy moments and fully enjoy them. Focus on filling your soul with the good of life and enjoy a good belly laugh that brings you to happy tears. Do not allow what has happened to rob you of the joyful moments of today. Find something everyday that brings a smile and laugh at something even if it yourself.

Trust God enough to enjoy the life God has given to you now. Smile more. It changes your attitude and outlook. Look for the joy. Look for the things that make you feel good inside. You will easily see the bad and negative because the world conditions you to see it. In this new life, focus on what brings you joy. You may have no clue so try out new experiences to see if you find joy in them. Joy is an inner peace and contentment. It is a warm feeling in your soul.

It is not being happy all the time because happiness is based on external circumstances and possessions. Joy comes from within our souls and laughter is a result of this joy. You release to God the heavy burdens of life and allow God to carry them. The lightness of the load produces an inner joy.

Laugh today. Find something each day that makes you laugh, smile, and soon joy begins to fill your soul.

• • • ● • ● • • • ·

Scripture

"Be full of joy in the Lord always. I will say again, be full of joy."
Philippians 4:6 NCV

Step

Laugh. Smile. Find Joy in Moments.

Pondering

It is good to pause in trying to figure out your next steps and just be happy.

Chapter Sixteen

Comfort

When Annie was sick, cold, or tired, she would wrap herself in the prayer quilt that my sister made for my husband, Dave. Annie quickly claimed it as her own after his death. She could literally cover herself completely with the blanket. I have pictures of her wrapped in it with only her nose sticking out. She felt safe and secure there, and the blanket gave her comfort.

In this different life, familiarity is still needed. While Annie adjusted well to all of my moves and adventures, she always had her blanket for comfort, and it provided her own safe space. Wherever I took her, she had a familiar towel or her blanket to lay on. She felt secure knowing this was her protected place. She usually fell asleep on it.

What gives you comfort? Comfort is a state of ease and a relief. You may have chosen some unhealthy things to comfort you during your loss and hurt – food, alcohol, shopping, TV, social media, gaming – all in excess. You may have used them as a way to escape the hurt and pain for a while. Certain foods are referred to as comfort food. It feels good to eat them and get lost in the taste, texture, and satisfaction.

Comfort is needed because of the feelings that are inside that bring discontent and uneasiness. Past hurts. Loss. Fear of the future. These bring discomfort. In this different life the past still enters when least expected. Sad moments are part of life no matter the focus. Days will come that you fall apart. It is okay to fall apart. Moments you just long for that familiar hug. Give yourself permission to feel the moments. Do not feel guilty that you need comfort. You just want life to feel better. It may seem difficult right now. It is finding healthy ways to meet the need of comfort. Comfort brings a sense of reassurance and eases your thoughts and feelings. Comfort gives you security and a sense that you are cared for and safe.

Music has brought comfort to me. I find songs that speak to my emotions and that lift me beyond the current pain. I listen to the words that speak to my soul and give me hope and see the light of eternity. Words that change my focus. I turn my eyes and heart to Jesus and the words bring comfort.

Movement has brought me comfort. Running, walking, biking. Keeping active releases the hurt, pain, and fears. It gets me out of the unhealthy comforts of food. On long bike rides, I find comfort in God's creation. I see the birds and wild animals. I see the beauty of the flowers and trees and sky, and I know God is with me and all around me. God gives comfort through the sounds of the birds. A cardinal gives me hope that I am not alone.

When I reach out to comfort another person on the journey, it brings hope and comfort to me. God comforts me with the same comfort He calls me to share with others. Sometimes just listening to another and understanding their pain and hurt and God using me to bring hope to them, gives me comfort and hope. I know I will make it. I have a purpose. My different life has meaning. I want to keep moving forward.

• • • • • • • • • •

Scripture

"God is the Father who is full of mercy and comfort. He comforts us every time we have trouble, so when others have trouble, we can comfort them with the same comfort God gives us." 2 Corinthians 1:3-4 NCV

Step

Find Comfort in Jesus

Pondering

Everything you go through helps to increase your trust and dependence on God. Focus on trusting God.

Chapter Seventeen

Being Pulled in Different Direction

Annie loved to walk in whatever neighborhood we lived. She usually walked fine on her leash. In the last area she lived, we walked down the street and would turn to the left to go up to the parking lot for an extended walk. Some days, Annie would try to pull me to the right side of the street to avoid going for the longer walk. She tried to convince me to take the shorter route. Annie would also pull me toward a smell or to chase a cat or squirrel. If I was not paying close enough attention, Annie would jerk on the leash and make me lunge forward unexpectedly. She was strong and could pull me in a direction I did not want to go.

I have allowed others to pull me in a direction that I did not want to go. Sometimes I let them do it before I realized it was not healthy or not what I wanted to do. I got stuck in pleasing others at the expense of myself. As I have attempted to find my new life, I got pulled into a new relationship out of the emotional pull of loneliness. I wanted adventure and thought that it would be a new experience and a different life. It was different, but not what either of us desired for our lives. We had different views of life and neither of us wanted to change. Just because it was what happened before and it was familiar, it does not make it healthy and good now.

If you mess up, own it, and move on. Do not allow others to define the life you are now living. They have not experienced what you have. It is the life God has given to you now. Your emotions pull you in so many different directions. Your friends and family will give you advise and suggestions on how to live your life, but they have not experienced the changes you have nor felt the loss and loneliness you have.

After my husband, Dave died, the condo felt like a hospice house and a place of death. It was filled with the possessions we had together, but I was no longer that person. I needed to change my environment. I made a drastic move and relocated to what was familiar – my hometown and siblings. It helped me regroup, rest, heal, write, and find my direction. I was pulled by family to stay, but my heart wanted something different. I was not ready to retire and settle. My move to my hometown gave me the opportunity to release most of my possessions and share them with my family. It gave me time to enjoy life in a comfortable and non-judgmental way. It gave me time to work through emotions and realize my priorities.

I was pulled back to another familiar, and I went back to where I had left but in a different location. I had released the material items of my past, but I was pulled to the familiar area again. But I learned to set clearer boundaries and define my passion and purpose. I got sidetracked for a period of time because of the emotional pull of loneliness and wanting companionship. I wanted to travel and enjoy adventures with someone. So I settled.

I accept I am one to learn lessons the hard way. All the directions I have gone have been learning and growing experiences. Most I will never repeat. To protect my heart, I was pulled into going back to my foundation for healing. I made choices quickly without considering all the consequences of these choices. I learned that I had to experience wrong directions and turn around so that I could help others on the path understand these choices and the consequences of them.

In this new life, repeating the past never works. God pulls you not just to replicate where you were going but to change directions and not be content trying to repeat the past. You cannot just delete someone from your life and replace that person with another and continue life as if there were no change. It does not work. You will be discontent and build resentment. It is also going a different direction in who you are now. You are no longer a couple and need to make decisions on your own. You will have different friendships, go different places, and find out what you like without the influence of another person.

Like Annie, sometimes we desire the familiar and easier route, but we may miss the adventures God has for us. It is taking the risk. Sometimes it is learning from what did not work. Accepting you made a wrong choice, ask for forgiveness, and go in a different direction. It is trying new ways of living. It is giving yourself permission to try and grace when your choice was not healthy. It is also keeping connected to God and not allowing distractions to take you off God's path.

• • • ● • ● • • • •

Scripture

"If you go the wrong way – to the right or to the left – you will hear a voice behind you saying, "This is the right way. You should go this way." Isaiah 30:21 NCV

Step

Take the Risk and Change Directions

Pondering

Sometimes you have to try things even if you are afraid. Take the risk.

Chapter Eighteen

No Plans

Annie never made plans for the day. She usually stayed in bed until I got out of bed. Later in life, I had to call her name to wake her up to go outside for her morning walk. After she ate, she would lay on her blanket and wait for me to take a shower and get dressed to see what I was going to do. Annie was always ready to go with me wherever I went except to the vet. She was always ready to enjoy the day whether it was being home with me or going on an adventure with me. When she jumped out of the vehicle wherever we were, Annie was excited about whatever was in front of her. She found joy in the people and the activity.

Planning and scheduling the day, the week, and the year is seen as an essential in our society. Taking charge and control of what is going to happen and making plans for every possible outcome so nothing surprises us is recognized as a sought after quality. Excessive planning and preparation cause anxiety and worry as fear enters that something will be forgotten, or someone will be upset. Planning states control is vital and always knowing what the day will bring is needed to have peace and to enjoy life.

I have always been a scheduler and planner because of my ministry and needing to have a calendar of events to coordinate with other ministries in the church. I have learned to put events on the calendar and not the emotions of the event so to lower worry and anxiety about the future event. I do not want to spend my time and thoughts in the future. Excessive planning and worry cause one to focus only on what is coming and not on what is currently happening in life.

Making plans with family and friends is good. Put the date on the calendar and release it to the future. Making plans for your own life is healthy when you also pray and release control to God and not just tell God to bless your plans. In this different life, I am learning to release plans to God and pray, "God if this is your will and direction for me...."

"People can make all kinds of plans, but only the Lord's plan will happen." Proverbs 19:21 NCV

I am also learning on days that I am not counseling to pray, "God, who do you want me to interact with today?" It is beginning the day with a clean slate and giving God control. It is depending more on God and trusting God with my life. As I move closer to God, I see the need to release control of not just my life but my schedule, my plans, my list and each day to God. I have felt such a relief that the day becomes what God has planned not me. I have said many times, "Ok, God, what do you want me to do today?"

Each morning I surrender myself and the day to God. Oh, I have tried to take the day back and plan it and usually anxiety and worry creep in and I feel that uneasiness in my stomach. I acknowledge – "Oops, Lord, I'm trying to take control again. Lord, today is yours, help me to listen to Your leading."

I have had to slow down, wait, listen, spend more time in God's Word and just be still and present with God. This different life for me is releasing all the control of doing and the tasks I think are important and have defined me in the past. It is giving control of my days and my life to God.

· · · ● · ● · ● · ·

Scripture

"I say this because I know what I am planning for you," says the Lord. "I have good plans for you, not plans to hurt you. I will give you hope and a good future." Jeremiah 29:11 NCV

Step

Give God Control of Your Day

Pondering

Allow God to lead you in today and each day of life's journey. Relax and give God the control. Everything is not on your shoulders – God's got it.

Chapter Nineteen

Fix Your Eyes

A nnie's eyes spoke volumes. She could stare at you like she was looking deep into your soul. Annie talked with her eyes. Most times her eyes were filled with love and joy. Through the journey of grief together, we spoke through our eyes to one another when I had no words. It was as if Annie got it and understood. When she would want another treat and I said, "No," her eyes would look at me almost demanding and we would have a stare down until Annie would surrender, lay down, and sigh.

I kept my eyes on Annie no matter where I took her, and she had to know where I was at all times, too. If I walked away, she usually came to find me. We fixed our eyes on each other. In times of loneliness, Annie's eyes were a comfort that someone was with me watching over me.

Annie's eyes also expressed pain. She did not whimper or cry much, but her eyes revealed the inner hurt. In her last moments of life, she licked my face as she lay on the table as if to say, "Thank you." Our eyes locked in that moment as she looked deep within me. As we fixed our eyes on one another, the love was expressed without words as our eyes said goodbye.

Annie taught me to keep my eyes fixed on the good part of life. She always knew where her love and support came from. She kept her eyes on me. She got distracted at times just like I do, but she always returned to me. The world has numerous distractions to catch the eye. It is easy to get lost if your focus is only on the problems, the fears, and the circumstances of life.

In this different life, my eyes have become fixed on Jesus. Jesus is the focal point of each day and moment. He looks deep into my soul and sees my heart and who I really am. Jesus loves me. Annie was not perfect, but she was mine. She was my faithful companion who always turned back to me in surrender when she had lost her focus on me. You, too, are not perfect and you get distracted, but when you turn your eyes back on Jesus, He loves you, forgives you, and calls you to keep moving forward with your eyes on Him.

I have learned what is really important in life – my relationship with Jesus. Like Annie, she learned our relationship was most important. All the other things did not bring her comfort, security, protection, and love. I have tried so many other things too, but in this different life, Jesus is all that truly satisfies. Instead of trying to fix yourself on others, fix your eyes on Jesus. When you fix your eyes on Jesus, your priorities align with His and you can release control and worry. You are not alone. God has you.

• • • • • • • • • • •

Scripture

"Let us fix our eyes on Jesus, the author and perfecter of our faith, who for the joy set before him endured the cross, scorning its shame, and sat down at the right hand of the throne of God." Hebrews 12:2 NIV

Step

Keep Your Eyes on Jesus

Pondering

Increase your attentiveness daily to God's Presence.

Chapter Twenty

Simplify

Annie had a quilted toy basket that contained all of her toys. She did not have an abundance of toys, and the majority were gifts given to her by family and clients. She would pull the stuffing out of the stuffed animal toys and still enjoy throwing them in the air and carrying them around. She had her favorites that she would bite a small hole in the corner of them or bite off an eye. It was like her mark on them to claim the toy as her own. She slept with her stuffed moose or rabbit many a night. I would clean out her basket and throw away the old beat-up ones. Her favorite toy was a simple sixteen-ounce empty plastic water bottle. She enjoyed unscrewing the lid with her teeth, taking off the plastic ring and crunching the bottle to make noise. It was simple, but Annie found joy in it. People would save bottles for her.

Life is complicated with so many decisions, directions, relationships, and responsibilities. So why complicate it more with an abundance of material possessions? With stuff! I like nice things and am blessed to have been born in the United States and have all the modern conveniences of water, bathroom facilities, electricity, and shelter. I give thanks to God for this privilege and blessing. Accumulating stuff and being surrounded by it can feel overwhelming and add to the lack of motivation to do anything in this different life.

Since I was a teenager, material possessions have not been a priority. After our family home was destroyed by fire when I was fourteen years old, I realized possessions are not as important as relationships. Things can be replaced. Life is simpler with just the essentials. Marriage changed that for me for a period of time especially being married to someone who loved to collect a wide variety of objects. But since his death, I have moved five times and purged what we had acquired together. I give away any extras. If I have not worn something in a season, it is donated. I go through my house each month and eliminate anything I have not used or no longer like or consider necessary. I am not a collector and have given away to family members the collectibles of my parents and grandmother so that they can now enjoy them.

When I simplified my possessions and the material part of my life, it became easier to simplify other parts of my life. Like I do not need to use my thought process to fix other people's lives. I have the privilege of allowing the Holy Spirit to speak through me, to listen to others and give suggestions, but I do not need to control or fix them. When I release this need, I simplify my thoughts and life and lower any anxiety I might have.

You carry around a lot of stuff in your head. In this new life, you need to ask yourself, "Does it really matter anymore?" Release the baggage of thoughts in your head that you have been holding onto for no real reason. Simplify your thinking. Quit rehearsing in your head all the hurts, injustices, wrongs done to you, your mess ups and sins, and the million other unnecessary thoughts. Forgive others and yourself and release the rest for God to deal with. Talk with God about your thoughts. Simplify your thoughts by focusing first on God and talking through everything with Him. When you start to worry and become anxious, give God those thoughts. This makes life more peaceful and content. Your thoughts go through God and He takes all the difficult ones and gives you the assurance He will walk you through whatever you are facing.

I simplify by not living in the future but in the present and focus on what is in today. I simply enjoy the moment and am fully present. I enjoy walks, nature, bike rides, music, laughter, and I look for God's presence around me. To simplify is not to live in comparison to others and try to keep up with what others have or do. It is simply being you. The one you are discovering and developing.

And with your words, be easily understood and straightforward. Be kind and direct that others understand and comprehend. This is a way to live simply.

I simply live with one main purpose – to please God. I simply care for what God has blessed me with and care for the people God puts on my path. I simply trust. I simply do good. I simply love God.

· · · · ● · ● · · · ·

Scripture

"My brothers and sisters, above all, do not use an oath when you make a promise. Don't use the name of heaven, earth, or anything else to prove what you say. When you mean yes, say only yes, and when you mean no, say only no so you will not be judged guilty."
James 5:12 NCV

Step

Uncomplicate Your Life

Pondering

You live in God's House. Everything is God's here on earth. You are His child. Just like when you were a child in your parents' home – everything was owned by them. They provided for you then as God provides for you now. Trust Him and release the stuff.

Chapter Twenty-One

Coming Closer

A nnie enjoyed meeting new people. She sometimes barked so they would acknowledge her presence. She always brought a toy to anyone who came to visit or rang the doorbell. Having a toy in her mouth stopped her barking and encouraged the person to come inside to play with her. Annie wanted the person to pet her and see her as part of the reason for the visit and to include her in the conversation. Some people ignored her, and Annie never pursued them but would turn to me for attention.

As I have tried new adventures and relationships, Annie has been accepting and tolerant of the changes. As long as I was there with her, she was fine. In this different life, some relationships have lasted for a season and concluded. You learn more about yourself and what you want for yourself in this new life, and do not need to stay where you do not have the freedom to be who you are.

Annie welcomed Ben into our lives very easily. She never barked at him but always brought a toy to him as if to say, "You are welcome here." As long as her routine did not change dramatically, she was fine with Ben. He came into her space and routine and that made her acceptance easier. Annie has taught me to find a life I enjoy and welcome others into it but not change it for them. This is not selfish; it is coming closer to who I am now and how I want to live the life God has given to me.

I am choosing who I draw closer to and who I release to be who they are in their own lives. Some of those who are in my different life were only minor characters in my previous life or who I did not know. It is creating new relationships with those who desire to take the adventure with me.

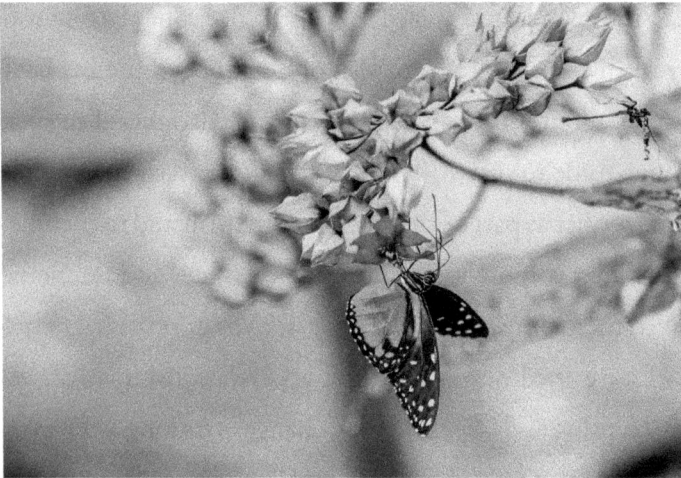

When one lives and experiences the moment, it is a true miracle. To be able to not worry or think about what happens next but to trust that God has the future and wants us to just find the purpose and the good in what is going on in front of us is a gift from God. Give yourself permission to live in the moment. Get out of your fear of what could happen and live in what is actually happening.

If you do not like it, you can either change the situation or your attitude toward it.

Life is what we create in our head. While the places I go are wonderful, and I experience the history, enjoy the entertainment, and breathe in the beauty of God's creation, I look for God appointments in these moments. It keeps me in the present because I am excited to see who God will put on my path today to reveal His love and presence. I know God is with me and all around me, but these special God appointments reveal that God has a purpose for me today and God will draw me even closer to Him through these encounters.

So when I live in the moment, I am more aware of the people around me. Someone I can encourage with a smile, praise for the work they are doing, thank them, or be open to listening to their heart. It is also being intentional about taking the time to bring people closer into my life and not be in such a hurry thinking that is out of my way or I will do it some other time. Make the call. Reconnect. Look around you with the eyes of Jesus. Encourage. Trust God to give you a Divine Appointment when you stay in the present moment with Him.

· · · · ● · ● · · ·

Scripture

"Let us draw near to God with a sincere heart and with the full assurance that faith brings, having our hearts sprinkled to cleanse us from a guilty conscience and having our bodies washed with pure water. Let us hold unswervingly to the hope we profess, for he who promised is faithful." Hebrews 10:22-23 NIV

Step

Look for God Appointments

Pondering

Find room for silence in your life so you can hear God's gentle whisper.

Chapter Twenty-Two

Get Used To Different

Annie adjusted to life without Dave because I was with her, and we literally spent most of our time together. We pulled closer to each other. In all our moves, Annie adapted to a new routine as long as she had her familiar bed, blanket, and toys. When she no longer had the stamina and endurance to run, it was more difficult for me to adjust to running without her. I was lonely, but she just slept during my run time. I felt a distance from her and did not want to leave her alone. She usually slept near the door until I returned. We adjusted.

Then Annie began to have bladder issues and needed to wear a diaper. The reality of her aging brought questions of how she would decline. What would this look like? Annie adjusted to the diaper and even learned to take it off when it bothered her, but she mostly took it in stride. Then her diabetes was diagnosed with a rapid decline. Annie just slept more, ate less, and needed comfort and touch even more. Life was different, but we adjusted. I had moved my office to my home months earlier and now understood how significant this was for Annie. She could stay in her home and still do her job as a therapy dog. It was different but worked out perfectly for both of us.

Then Annie died. God released her to Heaven. Annie was free from the restrictions and failures of her body. She was healed perfectly and running in Heaven. Annie and I got used to different together. Now I have had to get used to different without her.

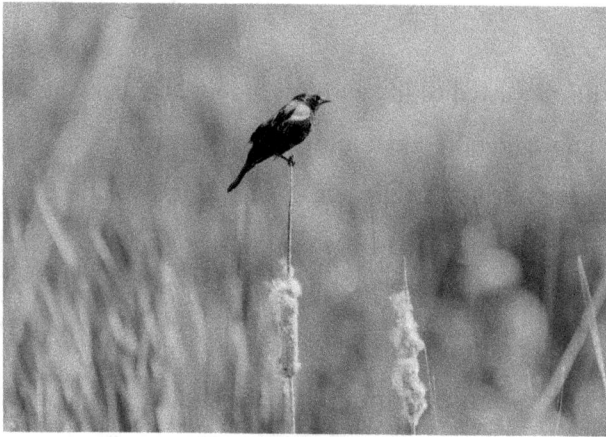

Through Annie and our time together, I learned that you cannot put your old life into this different life. You are different and how people relate to you is now different. No replacements. It is experiencing new adventures to see what you like now. I have been asked if I will get another dog. The answer is no. I cannot replace Annie just like you cannot replace a spouse, a child, a parent, a friend. There is a completion to that role and relationship.

Their love and legacy live on in each one of us. Our lives are not completed though. We need to live on in God's love and grace.

Now I am taking steps in this different life without Annie. I am so thankful for her and the life we shared together. She was my comfort and support during a difficult journey. But now she has given me a freedom I have never known. I am in a season where I can make my own ministry schedule and work when I choose.

Annie and God knew, I had someone that would now enjoy these new adventures with me, and Annie did not need to be the one to go with me anymore. I now have the freedom to travel and go anywhere I desire, and God leads me without worrying about leaving Annie or making arrangements for her care. That always weighed heavy on my heart when I had to leave her.

It was as if Annie wanted to make sure I was going to be OK with my new companion. She gave her approval. Her purpose was complete. She had earned her reward.

I am getting used to different. It is a freedom knowing that the old life is completed. It was good. It was what was fulfilling, and it was my purpose. I cannot live it again. I now try new experiences. Some I enjoy so much I want to do again, as for others, I am thankful I tried it. It is actually living, not just planning to someday. That is what this life is about now. If you want to do something, do it now. Do not put it on a list to do someday – a bucket list. Make the plan. Book the flight. Let go of the hurt. Stop trying to change someone. Choose who you want to spend time with and do it. Do not worry about how someone will see it. It is just you and God now.

Embrace Jesus who walks with you in this different. When you turn to Jesus and actually experience His presence, you find yourself living an abundant and full life. Live in the freedom you now have. You are free to choose your life – what you will do, where to go, what to eat, who to hang out with. Sadness keeps you chained to trying to re-live the past and stay confined to the old way that is empty and unfulfilling. Turn toward freedom. Learn to live life in a different way.

· · · ● · ● · ● · ·

Scripture

"Also, no one ever pours new wine into old leather bags. Otherwise, the new wine will break the bags, and the wine will be ruined along with the bags. But new wine should be put into new leather bags." Mark 2:22 NCV

Step

Live into the Different

Pondering

Trust God in all circumstances even when the path is difficult and different.

Chapter Twenty-Three

Look Up

A nnie was a dog that watched birds. She looked up into the sky when we walked. She would sit outside in the yard and watch the birds fly from tree to tree. If they got too close to her, she would bark. Annie did not like buzzards circling in the sky and would bark and run and jump. It was amazing how far up in the sky the buzzards could be, and she would still bark at them.

Annie always looked up when a person came to the house or office. She did not like people just standing because they were too far up for her to reach them or get petted. She wanted people to sit down so she could sit beside them and get attention.

In the last months of Annie's life, each evening she would lay in our living room area and look up at the front door and bark. She saw something. I have no idea what it was. Maybe it was an angel or someone preparing to be with her as she crossed over into Heaven.

Annie taught me to look up. See the beauty around me. See God's creation and glory. When we look down, we only see the problems, the dirt, what needs to be done. When we look up, we see what God created. The sunrise and the sunsets can only be seen when we look up. When we look down, we feel the sadness and despair of life.

When you look down – when you only see the brokenness, problems, and the hurt – life is painful and dreary like the dark clouds and rain. God does not always take away the storms, but He always promises to be with you through the storms of your life. Sometimes God even sends a sign like a rainbow reminding that He is with you and will do what He promised. God will walk you through the storm. You just need to look for Him. Where are you looking?

Many of you have been hurt by others breaking their promise to you. Others of you have prayed for healing and only received pain. You prayed for justice, and evil seems to keep winning. You cried out to God, and you still feel alone. Sometimes it is hard to look up and praise God. It seems easier to look down and muddle through life. When you focus on the hurt and pain, you stay in the darkness of the storm. It is difficult to trust in the storm, but that is what I keep trying to do.

I still trust the Lord to hold my hand because God has been faithful in the past. His Word promises that He will never leave me. He loves me and walks with me. Jesus gives me His Spirit to live within me. I know God has held my hand throughout my life. I trust God even when the storm is raging around me. Trust is more than how I am currently feeling. It is knowing God is with me even if I do not feel it. When I look up to the sky and let go of the earthly worries and struggles, I only see the light of God's presence.

You look down not just in the storms but in the dailyness of life. You get caught in a routine and sometimes it just becomes mundane and lifeless. Task after task. Work after work. Just getting by at times. You then focus on the negative, the loneliness and lack of fulfillment. You just look down and it creates a sadness and a wonder if this is all there is to life. Only when you look beyond the demands and emptiness of this world and look up to seek God's presence do you find life.

Look up from your focus of what is wrong, negative, and what has changed. This moment, the now, is the best moment of your life because it is what you have right now. Live in the now. What is good. Look up and see God. God has a purpose and calling in your life right now.

I am learning to look up more. Sometimes I see a rainbow, sometimes I see the blue sky and sunshine, sometimes I see the stars, and sometimes I see the darkness, the rain, and the clouds. But every time I look up, I trust that God is there. God wants me to focus on His presence. He wants me to trust Him, to hold His hand through the storms and through the pain and hurt, to hold His hand in the dailyness of life, and to look up and speak His name. Look up!

· · · ● · ● · · ·

Scripture

"I look up to the hills, but where does my help come from? My help comes from the Lord, who made heaven and earth." Psalm 121:1-2 NCV

Step

Look Up to God

Pondering

Live life in a responsive mode – looking for what God is doing and thanking Him.

Chapter Twenty-Four

Leave A Mark

Early in Annie's life at our home on Saylor Road, I had to keep Annie on a leash or wire line coated with plastic or she would run to the neighbor's farm. One day she was on her wire line, and we were working in the back yard. Annie's line was not fastened to a tree, but if she ran, the line was long enough that I could step on it and stop her. We were talking with the neighbors when Annie jerked on the line to run after their dog, and it wrapped around my ankle making it bleed. It left a burn mark, and I now have a permanent scar on my right ankle. Annie left her mark.

Annie also left her mark on my life and heart. Annie was a servant in her therapy dog role. She learned quickly to give support to those who were emotionally hurting. Annie sacrificed for me by being my emotional support through my grief. And in the end, she gave up her life so that I could be free of the responsibility of her care and find a new life and purpose. Annie left her mark of sacrifice, serving, and emotional support.

When Annie served, she focused on the emotions of others, and Annie received the blessing of being petted and getting belly rubs.

When you serve and care for others, it gets you out of yourself and focus on the needs of others. You also receive a blessing, and it fills you up. You do not serve for this reason. Annie did not serve just to receive. Annie leaves her mark of reaching out to others which fulfilled her purpose and gave meaning to her life.

Annie's life leaves a mark of trust. Annie trusted me completely. She was totally dependent upon me. She had her own unique personality that she never lost. In order to step into this different life, I need to trust my Master like Annie trusted me. I need to consistently trust Jesus. Trust is assured reliance. It is confidence and dependence upon God. It is taking a step into the darkness of this new life and having the hope that God's light will be revealed. Annie always knew I would be there for her. It is knowing God is always with you. No doubts.

Annie's life leaves her mark of love. Love never ends. It just takes a different form. Her unconditional love is part of me forever. Nobody can change it.

Annie leaves her mark of adventure. She was always willing to try something new or go with me even though she had no clue where I was going. Annie just lived in front of her. Never concerned about where I would take her as long as she was with me. I am learning to just go on life's adventure with God and be content wherever God takes me.

Annie was just herself. She never pretended to be anyone else. I tried to train her to be different, but she was content being herself. Be your unique self. Embrace who you are now. You can recreate yourself to be whomever you want to be. Do not settle for who you were or who somebody else wants you to be. Use your freedom to be who God created you to be.

Annie taught me to love adventure. Never be afraid to try something new or go somewhere you have never been. Annie's life became what she could never imagine considering her humble beginnings. I understand this from my own humble beginnings.

Find your new purpose in life. God has brought you to this new life. You have learned from the good and from difficult experiences. You have a foundation of faith. Go to this foundation and take steps toward living life right in front of you. God has begun a new work in you and a new path to follow.

•••••••••••

Scripture

"I remember your true faith. That faith first lived in your grand-mother Lois and in your mother Eunice, and I know you now have that same faith. This is why I remind you to keep using the gift God gave you when I laid my hands on you. Now let it grow, as a small flame grows into a fire. God did not give us a spirit that makes us afraid but a spirit of power and love and self-control." 2 Timothy 1:5-7 NCV

Step

Live. Love. Be You.

Pondering

Discover the gifts God has given you. Your purpose in life is to give them away.

Chapter Twenty-Five

Contentment

Annie was content to just be with me. It did not matter where we were as long as she was with me. In all the moves and places Annie and I lived, she always found her spot. In the last condo, she was most content in the sunroom where I counseled. Annie enjoyed the sunshine and the light from all the windows. If the door was closed to the sunroom, Annie would stand at the door and bark to go into the room even at night. She had found her space.

In this different life, it is finding your space in life. It is being happy in the life you now have, and being content with who you are and an acceptance of you as a person. This is now you. It is finding your happy place not just physically but also your emotional and spiritual happy place. One of my happy places in life is being in the sunshine. The sunshine warms my body and soul. I soak up the Vitamin D, and it brings a peace and calmness to me. It feels like God is warming my heart through the sunshine. The beach is my physical happy place which includes the sunshine, the sounds of the waves and water. It refreshes my soul.

Contentment is a state of happiness and satisfaction. It is not always an excited type of happiness but a peacefulness within you. It is an inner joy and sense of peace. You smile and are grateful for the moment. Being thankful is a vital part of contentment. It is coming to the acceptance that this is now my life and being grateful for the opportunity to live this new life. You are grateful for the small pleasures of life and your needs are satisfied.

Contentment does not mean that you will not experience problems, struggles, and heartaches again. It just means you are not controlled by your circumstances. It is being satisfied with the present. Contentment is an acceptance and appreciation of where you are now in life. You give thanks for everything around you and do not focus on what may be lacking.

Contentment comes with living in the present and enjoying what is around you. You cannot have contentment without gratitude. It is being grateful for your past but not being consumed by it nor trying to keep living in the past. The past is completed.

To be content in this different life is to live fully and abundantly in the present. It is appreciating what you have and where you are now in life. Embrace the past but do not dwell on it. Look to the future.

Contentment is a choice. You can choose to remain the victim of your past. You can choose to live in the past and only see and feel the hurt and pain. Or you can choose to be grateful for the life you now have and find peace in life. Peace only comes from the Prince of Peace, Jesus. Jesus promised to give His peace to all who come to him.

"I leave you peace; my peace I give you. I do not give it to you as the world does. So don't let your hearts be troubled or afraid." John 14:27 NCV

Contentment and peace is grounded in Jesus. It has very little to do with what is going on around you nor what you have acquired or lost in life. It is being fully present in the now and finding peace within your soul. It is knowing God will help you deal with whatever happens next. Chaos and the noise of the world tries to take away your peace wanting you to be anxious and afraid. Jesus wants you to receive His peace – an inner sense of the Holy Spirit's presence. Contentment means that you believe God has you each moment of your life. You are aware of God all around you.

Choose contentment. Choose to enjoy life. Choose to be happy. Choose joy. Choose the life you now have and live it fully. Take deep breaths and look around you. This is your life. Choose to be content.

· • • ● • ● • • • ·

Scripture

"I am not telling you this because I need anything. I have learned to be satisfied with the things I have and with everything that happens. I know how to live when I am poor, and I know how to live when I have plenty. I have learned the secret of being happy at any time in everything that happens, when I have enough to eat and when I go hungry, when I have more than I need and when I do not have enough." Philippians 4:11-12 NCV

Step

Find Your Peace and Contentment

Pondering

When you are dependent on God and aware of His constant Presence, you will find joy and abundant life – living life to its fullness now.

Conclusion

Wow! This is my life now. This is real. This is what I have now. It looks and feels different. I am excited about living and enjoying the new and different life most of the time. I get pangs of guilt that I am leaving behind the ones I have loved. I miss Annie and desire the joy she brought to me. I sit and remember and give thanks for her life and love. I am living in gratitude for those God allowed me to walk the journey of life. I am grateful to those who have directed me down the path of life and have been signposts to guide me. Annie has been a signpost of love, support, compassion, adventure, and has pointed me down a path that she cannot travel. She has given me the freedom to walk into this different life.

In this new life, live with the freedom you now have. You did not create it, but God allowed you this freedom and has given you the gift of a new life. So, no guilt, please. You are free to live boldly and abundantly. Accept and live your life to its full potential. Live in the today not just getting through the day. Stay present in the now. Focus on what is in front of you not on what comes next or what you think you need to do next. Enjoy what you are currently doing and be aware that God is with you. Draw closer to God. It is experiencing the now. Complete it, then focus on the next experience. One and done.

Simplify life. Release the thoughts of worry and measuring up to other people's standards and views. Be who God created you to be. If you do not like how life is right now, then choose to live differently. This is the only life you have now, and you are the one making the choices.

What if instead of wishing for the life you used to live and grieving over the past, you focused on the good of today. Your past is completed but not forgotten. It will always be a part of who you are, but it no longer has control over your future. Live in gratefulness to God for His blessings. Focus on what you have and who you are, not the negative what ifs of the past life.

Turn up the volume to God not the world, not other people. Look up more and say, "It's you and me, God." Believe that God has brought you through the valley. Not what you expected, but what happened. You were not punished nor were you meant to stay in the valley. You may never know the reason or the answer to the "why." You are on the other side looking forward to the horizon of your different life.

Embrace the change and enjoy each adventure! Live in these different moments. Live knowing God is with you. Breathe in the Holy Spirit and take in the moment right in front of you. Breathe in the freshness of this different life. Live Different Moments!

Steps Into This Different Life

1. Embrace Change. (Romans 8:28)

2. Depend on God. (Psalm 37:5)

3. Daily Movement. (Isaiah 40:31)

4. Let go and Let God. (Philippians 3:13-14)

5. Define your Space and Set Limits. (Exodus 19:23)

6. Feel the Freedom of Releasing. (Isaiah 61:1)

7. Trust God. *Accept yourself as you are.* (Proverbs 3:5)

8. Try New Experiences. (Psalm 119:35)

9. Build on Your Groundwork. (Corinthians 3:11)

10. Be Kind To Yourself. (Ephesians 4:1-2)

11. Step Into Who You Are Becoming. (Galatians 6:4-5)

12. Find a Balance for Life. (Proverbs 16:9)

13. Be Fully Present in the Now. (John 10:10)

14. Rest in God's Presence. (Matthew 11:28-30)

15. Laugh. Smile. Find Joy in Moments. (Philippians 4:6)

16. Find Comfort in Jesus. (2 Corinthians 1:3-4)

17. Take the Risk and Change Directions. (Isaiah 30:21)

18. Give God Control of Your Day. (Jeremiah 29:11; Proverbs 19:21)

19. Keep Your Eyes on Jesus. (Hebrews 12:2)

20. Uncomplicate Your Life. (James 5:12)

21. Look for God Appointments. (Hebrews 10:22-23)

22. Live Into the Different. (Mark 2:22)

23. Look up to God. (Psalm 121:1-2)

24. Live. Love. Be You. (2 Timothy 1:5-7)

25. Find Your Peace and Contentment. (Philippians 4:11-12)

About the Author

ELAINE J. CLINGER STURTZ is a retired elder in the United Methodist Church and a Licensed Professional Clinical Counselor (LPCC) in private practice. Elaine graduated from Otterbein University in Westerville, Ohio. She received her Master of Divinity and Master of Arts in Counseling Ministry from The Methodist Theological School in Delaware, Ohio. Elaine is the author of three devotional books – *Love Lighted Path, Glimpses of God, and The Final Dance of Life Our Journey With Judy*. She is the author of *Living In The Different* – the journey of grief and loss. Elaine wrote her fifth book on the legacy of her husband, Dave – *Life Lessons of a Lone Trooper*. Elaine is currently counseling, leading seminars and traveling with her new companion, Ben. Elaine writes a weekly blog and has a website – livinginthedifferent.com.

www.ingramcontent.com/pod-product-compliance
Lightning Source LLC
Chambersburg PA
CBHW060910280326
41934CB00007B/1259